Inventions of the 1700s

by Michael Burgan

Content Adviser: Melodie Andrews, Ph.D.,
Department of History,
Minnesota State University, Mankato

Reading Adviser: Rosemary G. Palmer, Ph.D.,
Department of Literacy,
College of Education, Boise State University

Compass Point Books ✦ Minneapolis, Minnesota

Compass Point Books
3109 West 50th Street, #115
Minneapolis, MN 55410

 This book was manufactured with paper containing at least 10 percent post-consumer waste.

On the cover: Color lithograph, Eli Whitney's Cotton Gin, operated by black slaves, 1793

Photographs ©: Private Collection/Peter Newark American Pictures/The Bridgeman Art Library, cover, 33; Prints Old and Rare, back cover (far left); Library of Congress, back cover, 20, 32, 36; Bettmann/Corbis, 4, 15, 38; Brian McEntire/Shutterstock, 6; North Wind Picture Archives, 8, 16, 24, 41; Nancy Carter/North Wind Picture Archives, 9, 37; Victorian Traditions/Shutterstock, 11; The Granger Collection, New York, 12, 18, 29, 35; Mary Evans Picture Library, 14, 26; Courtesy of the Banneker-Douglass Museum, Annapolis, Maryland, 19; The Print Collector/Alamy, 22; Liam Davis/Corbis, 23; Ramon Berk/Shutterstock, 27; Stock Montage/Getty Images, 28; Wikimedia, public-domain image, 31; Monticello/Thomas Jefferson Foundation, Inc., 34; National Archives and Records Administration, 40.

Editor: Matthew Bichler
Page Production: Ashlee Schultz
Photo Researcher: Svetlana Zhurkin
Cartographer: XNR Productions, Inc.
Library Consultant: Kathleen Baxter

Creative Director: Keith Griffin
Editorial Director: Nick Healy
Managing Editor: Catherine Neitge

Library of Congress Cataloging-in-Publication Data
Burgan, Michael.
  Inventions of the 1700s / by Michael Burgan.
      p. cm.—(We the people)
  Includes index.
  ISBN 978-0-7565-3638-1 (library binding)
  1. Inventions—United States—History—18th century—Juvenile literature.
  2. Inventors—United States—Biography—Juvenile literature. I. Title. II. Series.
  T48.B87 2008
  609.73'09033—dc22   2007032703

Visit Compass Point Books on the Internet at *www.compasspointbooks.com*
or e-mail your request to *custserv@compasspointbooks.com*

TABLE OF CONTENTS

A BETTER WAY TO WORK

With one simple invention, Eli Whitney changed history. In 1793, when he was visiting Savannah, Georgia, he heard about slaves separating seeds from raw cotton. A single slave spent a full day removing 1 pound (.45 kilograms) of

On many plantations, each slave was required to pick a certain amount of cotton, which could be hundreds of pounds, each day.

usable cotton from 3 pounds (1.35 kg) of cotton with seeds. Then someone came to Whitney with an idea. Perhaps a machine could separate seeds from cotton faster than a person could. Whitney soon designed such a machine, which he called a cotton gin.

By saving time in the separation process, Whitney's cotton gin allowed Southern farmers to produce more cotton than ever before. But as they grew more cotton, plantation owners bought more slaves. Whitney's cotton gin showed that some inventions have effects even their inventors cannot predict. Those effects are not always good for everyone involved.

At the beginning of the 1700s, most people did not have the time or the skill to create inventions. Most American colonists raised just enough crops for their families. Women made household goods such as the family's clothes, soap, and candles. Men made simple tools such as planes for smoothing wood. Few children received much schooling, and college was only for wealthy men.

Homemade candles were hung outside to allow the wax to cool.

Through the century, some Americans learned about science and technology, and a few had the creative spark of an inventor. They saw a way to do something faster, better, or more cheaply. Rather than creating something totally new, most inventors drew on the ideas of earlier inventors. American inventors sometimes looked to Europe for ideas and applied what they learned to conditions in America. Sometimes two inventors came up with the same idea at almost the same time. A group of people might work

6

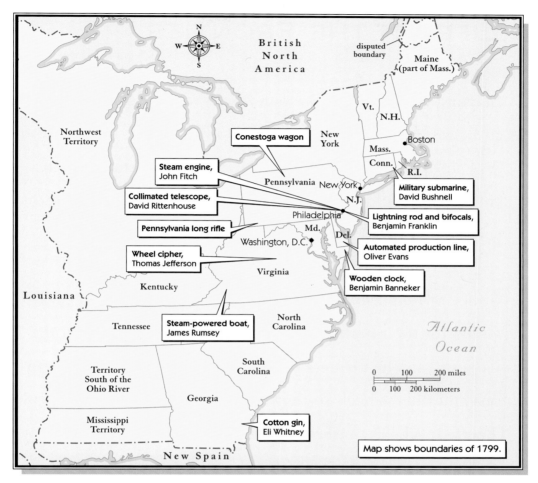

Pennsylvania was home to six major inventions of the 1700s.

together on an invention as well.

Eli Whitney and the other 18th century inventors changed the lives of all Americans—those living then and those living now.

7

LIFE ON THE FRONTIER

Starting in the 1680s, German immigrants began to settle in Pennsylvania. Many moved onto the frontier, where land was cheap and plentiful. But they found that traveling in these areas could be hard. Roads were usually narrow paths scattered with rocks and logs.

Around 1720, German farmers in the Conestoga Valley of Pennsylvania invented a kind of wagon that was suited for the rough land of the frontier. They called it the Conestoga. The farmers changed the shape of existing wagons and their wheels so they could carry goods more easily. The rear wheels on the biggest Conestoga wagons were almost 6 feet (1.8 meters) tall. These large wheels helped the wagon roll over rocks and logs in the road. The wagon itself was shaped like a boat, and its bottom was sealed to keep out water. When farmers came to a stream or small river, they could safely cross without getting their cargo wet. The front and back of the wagon's floor curved up slightly, so the cargo would not slide when the wagon went up and down hills.

With their Conestoga wagons, farmers could take crops to market and bring home goods they could not make themselves. The wagons were pulled by up to eight horses or oxen. The Conestoga was common in Pennsylvania and nearby colonies until the mid-1800s. By then, as Americans moved west to the Pacific Coast, they created a smaller

Replicas of the Conestoga wagon are still built today to show people what travel was like in the 18th century.

version of the Conestoga that could be pulled by only two horses or oxen. These "prairie schooners" took many families to their new homes in the West.

In the early 1720s, German immigrants in Pennsylvania developed a rifle with a longer and narrower barrel than the ones that had been used in Germany since the

To travel across streams and rocky paths, settlers had to design a better wagon.

In the mid-1800s, moving west was easier with a prairie schooner, but the trip was still long and dangerous.

1460s. Like the German rifles, these guns had a spiral groove cut inside their barrels. This groove helped the metal balls used as bullets travel farther and straighter than balls shot from guns with smooth barrels. The new Pennsylvania gun was easier to handle than the German rifles. It was soon named the Pennsylvania long rifle. Although first used for hunting, these rifles became important weapons during the French and Indian War as well as the American Revolution.

11

FAMOUS EARLY INVENTORS

The developers of the Conestoga wagon and the Pennsylvania long rifle are unknown today. But by the middle of the 1700s, Americans began keeping better records of inventors and inventions.

In Pennsylvania, Benjamin Franklin made a name for himself as a scientist. His most famous experiments involved electricity. He discovered that electricity has negative and positive charges. In 1752, he showed that electricity exists in the atmosphere.

Franklin was a publisher as well as a scientist, and each year he published a book called *Poor Richard's Almanac*. In the 1753 edition, he wrote that he had discovered "the means of securing … [homes] and other Buildings from Mischief by Thunder and Lightning."

Franklin had discovered that pointed metal objects attract electricity. He proposed putting a pointed metal rod on the roofs of buildings. A wire connected the rod on the

Benajmin Franklin tested various kinds of lightning rods. He discovered that sharp rods worked better than blunt ones, and metal worked better than wood.

13

roof to a rod buried in the ground. Instead of hitting the building, the lightning struck the rod on the roof. The electricity then traveled down the wire to the rod in the ground and was distributed into the dirt.

Franklin also made practical improvements to existing inventions. Italian monks had invented the first form of

Experiments did not always take place in a lab or workshop. For example, Benjamin Franklin experimented with electricity outdoors.

14

Much of what is known today about inventions was learned by reading the inventors' letters.

eyeglasses at the end of the 13th century. Franklin wore one pair of glasses to see things far away and another to read. He grew tired of switching from one pair to the other and had his eye doctor cut the lenses of both pairs in half. His

15

Franklin often made models of his inventions, such as his Pennsylvania fireplace, before creating the real thing.

doctor then placed half of the distance lens in the top of the frame and half of the reading lens in the bottom. Franklin had created a new type of glasses: bifocals.

Franklin also created a way to heat homes more efficiently. Fireplaces at the time were the only sources of heat in a home, and they only heated the air right in front of the fire. He believed cold drafts led to poor health, so he designed and built a new kind of fireplace. His Pennsylvania fireplace filled an entire room with warm air. Franklin knew warm air rises, so he made a hole above the flames

16

where the warm air left the fireplace and entered the room. That air slowly sank as it cooled a bit, and warmer air from the fire took its place. The sinking air, however, was still warm enough to heat the room. Franklin later adapted his fireplace to be a stove. Made of cast iron, it sat in the middle of a room and sent out heat in all directions. The basic design of the Franklin stove is still used today.

Franklin's interest in science and inventing inspired another Philadelphian, David Rittenhouse. Like Franklin, he had a wide range of interests and was self-taught. By 1750, when he turned 18, Rittenhouse had built his first clock. Rittenhouse also built telescopes and devices called orreries. Driven by clockworks (the gears inside clocks), orreries show how the positions of the planets change over time. Thomas Jefferson called him "second to no astronomer living." Later Rittenhouse invented the collimated telescope. Collimated means that the lenses inside the telescope were aligned in a precise way that gave the viewer a sharper image than did previous telescopes. Rittenhouse also designed and improved telescopes used by surveyors to locate land boundaries. His telescopes were smaller than existing ones, while just as accurate.

A skilled astronomer and mathematician, Benjamin

From 1791 to 1796, David Rittenhouse served as president of the American Philosophical Society, a group that promotes the study of sciences and humanities.

18

Banneker was a free African-American who lived in Maryland. After borrowing a watch from a friend, Banneker took it apart and made drawings of its gears and other workings. He then assembled a clock based on those drawings, carving the pieces out of wood. This was the first wooden clock made in America, and it kept accurate time for several decades.

In 1791, Benjamin Banneker wrote a letter to Thomas Jefferson. He asked Jefferson to give freedom and equality to black slaves.

WARTIME INVENTOR

When the American Revolutionary War began in 1775, Connecticut inventor David Bushnell turned his thoughts to the military. Great Britain had more money and a larger army than did the Americans. The colonies needed new weapons in their fight for independence. To help Americans attack British ships, Bushnell designed the first military submarine.

Even before the war, Bushnell had begun thinking

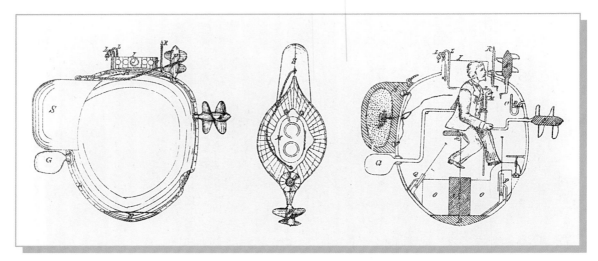

David Bushnell drew a sketch of his military submarine. Many inventors design their inventions on paper before building them.

about using explosives under water. In 1771, he put gunpowder in wooden kegs and used clocks as timers to trigger an explosion. These kegs were used as the first underwater mines. He realized submarines could be used to place the mines under enemy ships. A drill on the sub could be used to make a hole in the bottom of the ship, where a mine could be attached.

The first submarine had been invented in Europe in 1620, but Bushnell was the first to use one during wartime. With help from his brother Ezra, Bushnell built his sub in 1775. As he later wrote, the vessel "bore some resemblance to two upper tortoise shells of equal size, joined together." The sub was later known as the *Turtle*. The *Turtle* held just one person. This pilot had about 30 minutes of air to breathe. To move the sub, the pilot turned several oars. An oar shaped like a screw moved the vessel forward and backward. Two straight oars moved the sub up and down.

On the night of September 6, 1776, the Americans put the *Turtle* into battle. In New York Harbor, a volunteer

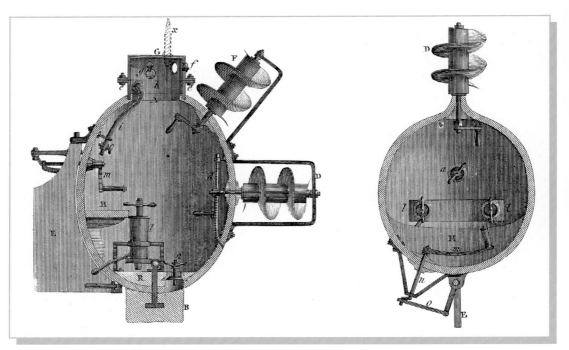

Instead of using a motor or engine, the Turtle *moved by the strength of the pilot.*

piloted the *Turtle* under the British ship *Eagle*, but he could not attach the explosive to it. The *Turtle*'s drill hit a metal bar on the bottom of the ship. Running out of air, the volunteer brought the *Turtle* back to the surface. He released the mine and it exploded, but the *Eagle* was not damaged. The Americans tried at least once more to use the sub to blow up a British ship but failed again. The British later claimed to have destroyed the *Turtle* by sinking a U.S. ship

Some replicas of the Turtle *weigh up to 2 tons (1.8 metric tons).*

that was carrying the sub. The Americans claimed they
took the sub ashore and took it apart so the British could
not capture it. In any case, Bushnell continued to build
naval mines to attack British ships.

THE STEAM ERA

After winning independence, Americans turned to rebuilding their economy and increasing the area in which they could live. Several talented inventors became interested in the steam engine. After English inventors perfected the engine, it eventually replaced animals and moving water as a source of power. Several Americans thought steam engines could also be used to power ships and land vehicles.

One morning in 1785, John Fitch watched a horse-drawn carriage roll by as he traveled on foot. He later wrote, "What a noble thing it would be if I could have such a carriage without the expense of keeping a horse." The solution, Fitch thought, was a steam-powered vehicle. He decided to build a boat rather than a carriage. With the help of his friend Henry Voight, Fitch built a steam-powered boat.

Steam engines require fuel, such as coal or wood. Fitch burned wood to heat water in a metal boiler. The steam produced by the boiling water created pressure that

24

Using horses to pull a carriage was expensive. Feeding, sheltering, and grooming the horses, as well as keeping them healthy, took a lot of time, money, and effort.

moved a piston up and down. The piston moved a series of oars through the water, propelling the boat. Fitch successfully tested the world's first steamboat in August 1787.

Over several years, he improved the boiler and replaced the oars with a paddle wheel. By 1790, Fitch offered the world's first steam-powered ferry service. His ferry could move up and down rivers at about 7 miles

John Fitch's first steamboat was propelled by oars much like those in a rowboat.

(11.2 kilometers) per hour. The trip was faster than on a sail-
boat, but not as quick as a fast horse pulling a carriage over a
smooth road. Fitch's ferry service soon went out of business.

James Rumsey had also been working on a steam-
powered boat. In 1785, President George Washington
backed Rumsey's plan to build a steamboat to travel on the

Potomac River. Washington said Rumsey's idea was so simple that "when seen and explained, [it] may be [carried out] by the most common mechanic."

Rumsey favored an idea that Benjamin Franklin had envisioned—jet propulsion. Today's jet planes have a similar technology using streams of hot air for power. For his boat, Rumsey set up a steam engine that powered a pump that forced out a powerful stream of water at the rear of the boat. The force of the water moving backward from the

Modern fighter jets are propelled by streams of hot air.

boat pushed the vessel forward. Rumsey tested his boat in December 1787 on the Potomac River. The boat reached a speed of 4 miles (6.4 km) per hour before the engine quit.

Rumsey and Fitch competed to receive patents for their steamboats. At that time states issued their own patents for inventions. In 1790, the U.S. government created a national patent office. Receiving a patent gave an inventor legal ownership of an invention or new process. Inventors could charge money for allowing others to build or use their patented inventions anywhere in the United States.

Today many people see Robert Fulton as the "father" of the steamboat. In 1807, he began the first successful

Robert Fulton was not only a talented inventor but also a gifted painter.

Robert Fulton's steamboat traveled up the Hudson River to Albany.

29

passenger service with a steamboat. But the work of Fitch and Rumsey, as well as European inventors, paved the way for Fulton.

Steam also interested Oliver Evans, an inventor in Delaware. Like Fitch, Evans saw the value of using steam to power vehicles. He designed a steam engine that used high pressure instead of the low pressure used in the first engines. Evans' engines were smaller and more powerful than the ones before them. But his greatest invention during the 1700s was the automated production line.

Before Evans and his creation, turning raw wheat into flour took the work of several strong men, and the flour was often unclean. Evans noted that a "great quantity of dirt … from the dirty feet of everyone who trampled" the grain became mixed in with the flour. In the early 1780s, Evans began designing a mill that could produce flour more quickly, cheaply, and cleanly than the old methods. His production line required only one worker to operate it.

Evans used rushing rivers as his power source.

Waterwheels were often used at mills of various kinds. In the basic design, water flowed over flat paddles on the wheel, forcing the wheel to turn. The wheel was attached to a rod. As the wheel turned, the rod moved a gear, which then turned the stone that crushed the grain.

In 1795, Oliver Evans published a book on automated mills.

In Evans' design, the turning waterwheel also powered large belts that moved over round wheels called pulleys. The belts moved through the mill. Buckets or cups attached to the belts carried the grain to the top of the mill. Gravity and other belts carried the grain through the factory and into machines where it was ground into flour.

31

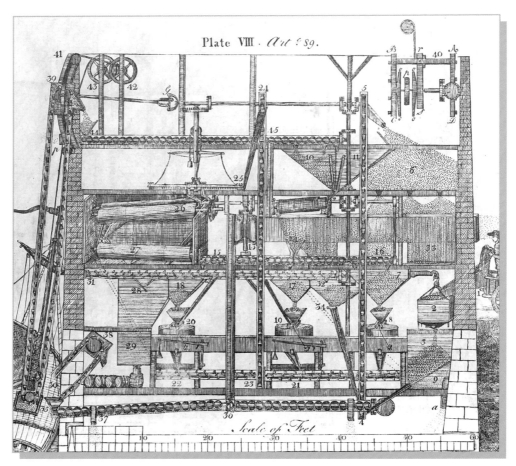

In the automated milling process, one worker dumped in the grain at the beginning and picked up the flour at the end. The mill did everything in between.

The process worked so well that other millers had Evans build similar mills for them. One of Evans' customers was George Washington.

INVENTORS IN THE SOUTH

When George Washington was elected the first U.S. president in 1789, he chose Thomas Jefferson of Virginia to be his secretary of state. Jefferson had written the Declaration of Independence in 1776. He was also a skilled inventor.

While he was secretary of state, advising the president on foreign affairs, Jefferson developed a new way to send secret codes. He wanted to send messages to President Washington that other people could not read. Jefferson developed a wheel cipher, a device that used

Thomas Jefferson served as the third U.S. president.

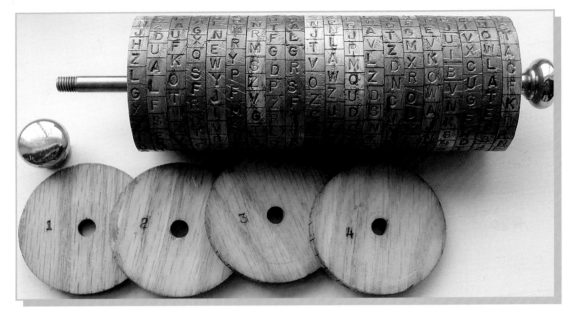

The wheel cipher was small, which made it easy to use anywhere.

wheels that turned on a peg. Each wheel had the 26 letters of the alphabet carved on it. Jefferson could turn the wheels to spell out a message. Then he would look at another line above or below his message, which would show a random group of letters. He would copy down those letters and send them out. The person receiving the message would have a wheel cipher as well. He would line up the random letters, then look for the one line of letters around it that spelled out a readable message.

34

Over the years, Jefferson also improved several existing inventions. One was the farmer's plow. The plow then in use had a moldboard, a wooden part that pulled up the earth that was cut by a blade. Jefferson created a new moldboard that moved through the earth much more easily. He also improved a device that let him copy messages as they

Thomas Jefferson made some of his inventions, like his copying machine, for his personal use before introducing them to the public.

were being written. It held two pens, so he could write two copies of a letter at once.

In Georgia, Eli Whitney invented a machine that changed the economy of the Southern states. Whitney came to Georgia from Connecticut in 1793, on his way to a teaching job in South Carolina. He stayed at the Savannah farm of Catherine Greene. During his visit, Whitney showed a skill for making and repairing household items.

One day, some of Greene's friends talked about the difficulty of picking out seeds from cotton. The kind of cotton that grew in Georgia had sticky seeds.

Eli Whitney attended Yale and graduated at age 28 despite having had little formal education as a child.

36

This made the process of separating seeds from cotton more difficult than with other kinds of cotton. Greene is supposed to have said, "Gentlemen, apply to my young friend,

Thousands of seeds were picked out by hand to get a small amount of cotton.

37

Eli Whitney designed a machine that made separating cotton from its seeds easier.

Mr. Whitney. He can make anything."

In just 10 days, Whitney created a gin—short for "engine"—that could separate the seeds from the cotton.

38

The machine used a small, rolling drum called a cylinder. Attached to the cylinder were wooden hooks that pulled the lint—the raw material to be spun into yarn—away from the seeds. At the same time, a piece of metal held the seeds in place.

This first cotton gin did not work as well as Whitney had hoped. Sometimes the cleaned cotton jammed it. He then replaced the hooks with wire spikes and added a brush that cleared away the cleaned cotton. Turning the small cylinder on the gin by hand, one person could now do the work of 10. Even more cotton could be cleaned in a day with larger models powered by horse or waterwheel. Soon Southern farmers began planting more cotton and buying more slaves to produce it.

In 1794, Whitney received a patent for his cotton gin, but historians argue that many people played a part in creating this machine. Some suggest that Greene gave Whitney ideas for the gin, such as using metal spikes. Others say Whitney got his idea for the gin after watching enslaved

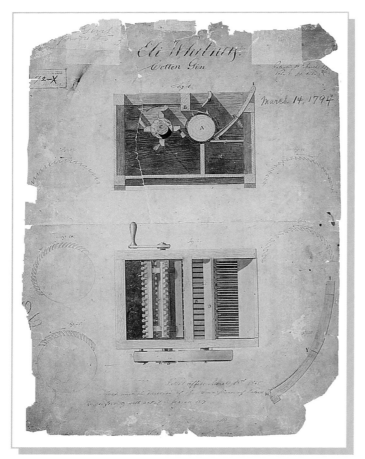

Inventors submitted drawings of their inventions to the patent office when applying for a patent.

workers use combs and other hand tools to remove the seeds. Several years before Whitney reached Georgia, Hogden Holmes of South Carolina began working on a cotton gin that used a row of metal saws to separate the seeds and cotton, rather than spikes. Holmes received a patent for his version of the gin in 1796.

As the young United States grew, the number of inventions grew along with it. The 19th century would see the invention of the mechanical reaper, the typewriter, and

In 1834, Cyrus Hall McCormick patented the mechnical reaper, which cut grain.

the telephone. The 20th century produced the FM radio, the microwave oven, and the cellular telephone. That spirit of invention continues today.

GLOSSARY

automated—done with the help of machines

cipher—device or method for concealing a message

economy—the way a country or region produces, distributes, and uses its money, goods, natural resources, and services

immigrants—people who move from one country to live permanently in another

mines—explosive devices that are concealed underground or underwater

patents—the rights to be the only person to make, use, or sell an invention for a certain number of years

piston—round part that moves up and down in an engine's cylinder

propulsion—driving force that moves something

pulleys—wheels with grooves cut into their edges that are used to move objects

DID YOU KNOW?

- Besides inventing the cotton gin, Eli Whitney developed a faster method of making guns. In 1812, his factory produced 15,000 guns for the U.S. government.

- The first U.S. patent was awarded in 1790 to Samuel Hopkins. He created a new way to make potash, a chemical used to help plants grow. Since then, the U.S. government has issued more than 7 million patents.

- All of the early records of U.S. patents were destroyed in 1836 during a fire at the Patent Office. Officials were able to recover copies of some of the records from private citizens.

- David Rittenhouse improved Benjamin Franklin's stove by adding an L-shaped pipe to it. The pipe drew air into the stove to keep the wood burning, then carried the smoke to the chimney.

- Like Hogden Holmes and James Rumsey, Benjamin Hanks and Abel Buell are often-forgotten inventors of the 1700s. Hanks designed a wind-powered clock and a corn-planting machine, and Buell invented a gem-polisher and a coin-making machine.

43

IMPORTANT DATES

Timeline

1720s	First Conestoga wagons and long rifles appear in Pennsylvania.
1744	Benjamin Franklin invents the Pennsylvania fireplace.
1753	Franklin describes the use of the lightning rod.
1776	David Bushnell launches his *Turtle*, the first submarine used during wartime.
1780s	Oliver Evans builds the first automated mill.
1787	John Fitch tests the first successful steamboat.
1790	The U.S. Patent Office opens.
1790s	Thomas Jefferson invents a wheel cipher.
1794	Eli Whitney receives a patent for his cotton gin.

IMPORTANT PEOPLE

DAVID BUSHNELL (1742–1824)

Connecticut native who studied explosives while attending Yale College; when the American Revolutionary War began, he invented the first submarine used during war, though it failed in its missions to blow up British warships; Bushnell also developed effective mines

OLIVER EVANS (1755–1819)

A skilled inventor, Evans used water power, belts, and pulleys to build the first automated mill; he also improved the design of steam engines, making them more powerful, and created the first working steam-powered land vehicle

BENJAMIN FRANKLIN (1706–1790)

Most famous as a writer and political leader, Franklin strongly supported American independence from Great Britain; he was also a scientist and inventor; his inventions include bifocal glasses, the lightning rod, the Pennsylvania fireplace, and the Pennsylvania stove

ELI WHITNEY (1765–1825)

Going to Georgia to teach, Whitney helped perfect a cotton gin that could quickly remove seeds from cotton; his invention greatly increased cotton production in the South

WANT TO KNOW MORE?

More Books to Read

Gibson, Karen Bush. *The Life and Times of Eli Whitney*. Newark, Del.:
    Mitchell Lane Publishers, 2007.

Masters, Nancy Robinson. *The Cotton Gin*. New York: Franklin Watts, 2006.

Stefoff, Rebecca. *Colonial Life*. New York: Benchmark Books, 2003.

Streissguth, Thomas. *Benjamin Franklin*. Minneapolis: Lerner Publications, 2005.

On the Web

For more information on this topic, use FactHound.

1. Go to *www.facthound.com*

2. Type in this book ID: 0756536383

3. Click on the *Fetch It* button.

FactHound will find the best Web sites for you.

On the Road

U.S. Patent and Trademark Museum

Madison Building

600 Dulany St.

Alexandria, VA 22313

571/272-0095

National Inventors Hall of Fame Museum

221 S. Broadway St.

Akron, OH 44308-1505

330/762-4463

Look for more We the People books about this era:

The Articles of Confederation

The Battle of Bunker Hill

The Battle of Saratoga

The Battles of Lexington and Concord

The Bill of Rights

The Boston Massacre

The Boston Tea Party

The Declaration of Independence

The Electoral College

Great Women of the American
*   Revolution*

The Minutemen

Monticello

Mount Vernon

Paul Revere's Ride

The Second Continental Congress

The Surrender of Cornwallis

The U.S. Constitution

Valley Forge

A complete list of We the People titles is available on our Web site:
www.compasspointbooks.com

INDEX

About the Author

Michael Burgan is a freelance writer of books for children and adults. A history graduate of the University of Connecticut, he has written more than 100 fiction and nonfiction children's books. For adult audiences, he has written news articles, essays, and plays. Burgan is a recipient of an Educational Press Association of America award.